THE MOOSE

BY
MARK E. AHLSTROM

EDITED BY
DR. HOWARD SCHROEDER

**Professor in Reading and Language Arts
Dept. of Elementary Education
Mankato State University**

PRODUCED AND DESIGNED BY
BAKER STREET PRODUCTIONS
Mankato, MN

CRESTWOOD HOUSE
Mankato, Minnesota

LIBRARY OF CONGRESS CATALOGING IN PUBLICATION DATA

Ahlstrom, Mark E.
  The moose.

  (Wildlife, habits & habitat)
  SUMMARY: Describes the physical characteristics, habits, and natural environment of the moose, the largest species of deer in the world.
  1. Moose--Juvenile literature. (1. Moose) I. Schroeder, Howard. II. Baker Street Productions. III. Title. IV. Series.
QL737.U55A355   1985   599.73'57   85-26931
ISBN 0-89686-279-8 (lib. bdg.)

International Standard Book Number:	Library of Congress Catalog Card Number:
Library Binding 0-89686-279-8	85-26931

ILLUSTRATION CREDITS:

Caron Pepper/Tom Stack & Assoc.: Cover
Lynn Rogers: 5, 6, 16, 29, 32, 40
Jeff Foott/Tom Stack & Assoc.: 9
Rick McIntyre/Tom Stack & Assoc.: 11
Stephen Krasemann/DRK Photo: 12, 24-25, 39
Phil & Loretta Hermann: 15, 21
Johnny Johnson/DRK Photo: 19, 22, 26, 31, 36, 42-43
Wayne Lankinen/DRK Photo: 35

CRESTWOOD·HOUSE

Hwy. 66 South, Box 3427
Mankato, MN 56002-3427

TABLE OF CONTENTS

INTRODUCTION:

A funny-looking horse

I had been up all night fishing for walleyes. It was the middle of May, and I was fishing on a lake near the northern border of Minnesota. I had been lucky. By the time it started to get light, I had caught five nice walleyes. One more fish and I would have my legal limit.

I decided to set the motor on the boat at a slow speed and slowly troll along the shore back to the cabin. As I set off, the sun was just coming over the treetops. A thin layer of fog drifted across the water. The fog made everything a bit hazy, but I didn't care. In fact, I was enjoying the "light show" that the fog and the sunrise were giving me. Every few seconds there was something new to look at. It was a great morning to be alive!

As I was getting near the cabin, I remember looking towards the foggy shore. I was looking for a white birch tree that leaned out over the water. I knew that I had to make a left turn at the birch tree. It would then be a short trip across a narrow part of the lake into the bay where the cabin was.

4

I didn't see the birch tree, but I could just barely see something standing in the water near the shore. As I got closer, it looked like a horse. Then I saw a small animal standing next to the large one. "Oh, neat," I thought. "A mare and her foal having a morning drink of water."

About the same time I began to wonder what horses would be doing on this lake. The lake was in the middle of the Superior National Forest. There weren't any farms for many miles in any direction. It was then that I noticed that the large animal had a very long nose. No horse had a nose like that! This "horse" didn't have the right kind of tail, either. There was just a short stub where a long, flowing tail should be. It was a very funny-looking horse.

Is it a horse?

"Wow," I said in a loud whisper when I realized what I was seeing. It was a cow moose and her calf. They were the first moose I had seen in the wild.

By now, I was just passing the animals. They were no more than thirty yards (27.4 m) from me. The motor was still running. "What's going on here," I wondered. "Wild animals are supposed to be afraid of people. These moose are just staring at me. I've heard some people say that moose are dumb, but this is silly."

A cow and her calf stand on the edge of a lake. These moose have unusual markings on their legs.

I kept going. I didn't dare shut off the motor. I thought that getting rid of the steady "putt-putt" of the motor might scare the moose.

I was quite a ways past the moose when the cow gave a quiet grunt. In an instant, the cow and her calf were off and running! They ran into the woods next to the lake and were soon out of sight. All I heard was some loud crashes as they ran off.

A short while later I spotted the white birch tree, and turned left. As I went across the lake, I thought about what had happened. About the only thing I figured out was why the moose had run when they did. I remembered that the wind was blowing into my face as I came up to the moose. This meant that the moose could not smell my human scent. As soon as I got past the moose a ways, the wind blew my scent towards them. That's what caused them to run off in a hurry.

But why didn't they run when they heard the motor, or saw me? It didn't make sense. When I got to the dock at the cabin, I decided that it was time to find out more about these strange looking animals.

Let's take a look at some of the things I learned.
— M.E.A.

CHAPTER ONE

The moose came from Asia

The moose is a member of the deer family. This group of animals is called the *Cervidae* family by biologists. There are more than fifty species, or types, of deer found around the world.

The experts believe that the history of the deer family began a very long time ago in Asia. The first deer were quite small. Some of them were no bigger than a house cat! These little deer didn't yet have antlers. They had tusks to help fight their battles. Over thousands of years the deer changed. Most of them slowly got larger and lost their tusks. Their needs had changed as they moved into new areas of the world. Many members of the deer family began to grow large antlers.

Like many other wild animals, many kinds of deer migrated to North America across the Bering Land Bridge. This narrow strip of land once joined Asia with what is now Alaska. At some point in time, the oceans rose and covered the land bridge. The deer adapted very well to their new homeland. They soon spread across all areas of North America.

The world's largest deer

Today, there are members of the deer family living all over the world. There are five main species of deer living in North America. They include the whitetail deer, the mule deer, the caribou, the elk, and the moose. The moose is the largest North American deer. In fact, it is the largest member of the deer family in the world.

The moose is the largest member of the deer family.

The moose is also found in northern Europe and Asia. In that part of the world, the moose is known as an elk. It was given the name long before the first explorers came to North America. These early explorers were not experts on animals. They thought that any large animal with big antlers should be called an elk. When they first saw animals that fit that description in the New World, they called them elk. Before long all the new settlers were calling these animals elk. What these people didn't know was that this animal already had a name. The same animal was found in Europe, where it was called a red deer.

Things got more confused when the settlers started seeing another large animal with antlers. This animal was much larger and its antlers were even bigger. The settlers knew that they couldn't call both animals an elk. Because the smaller of the two animals was already known as an elk, they came up with a new name for the bigger animal. The Indians called this large deer a *musee,* which was their word for "wood eater." In the English language, this word became moose.

The confusion remains to this day. In Europe, the world's largest deer is still known as an elk. In North America it is still called a moose. The second largest deer in the world is still called a red deer in Europe, and an elk in North America. The animals are the same. Just the names are different.

The Indians called this large deer "musee."

The moose in North America

Most experts now believe that there are three sub-species, or types, of moose in North America. The official name that covers all three types is *Alces alces.* The main difference is size. Moose follow a common law of nature. This law says that the colder the climate in which an animal lives, the larger it is likely

The largest moose live in the coldest climates.

to be. A larger body holds heat better than a smaller body. This allows the animal to adapt to its habitat.

The Alaskan moose is the largest subspecies. This type is found in Alaska and the Yukon. A bull, or male, moose of this type may weigh as much as eighteen hundred pounds (818 kg). The largest bulls will stand ninety inches (2.3 m) tall at the shoulder.

The smallest subspecies is the Shiras, or Wyoming, moose. This moose is found in the Rocky Mountains of Wyoming, Montana, Utah, Idaho, and southeastern British Columbia. Bulls of this type seldom weigh more than twelve hundred pounds (545 kg). The largest bulls will be about seventy inches (1.8 m) tall at the shoulder.

The most common subspecies is the Canada moose. This type is found all across the southern half of Canada. Its range then spreads north into the Northwest Territories and parts of the Yukon. This type is also found in the northern parts of Minnesota, Michigan, and Maine. The largest bulls weigh about fourteen hundred pounds (635 kg), and are around eighty inches (2 m) tall at shoulder height.

The cows, or females, of each type will usually weigh about one-fourth less than the bulls, and they will not be as tall. All moose are about one hundred inches (2.6 m) long, from the tip of their nose to their short tail. The tail is only about three inches (7.7 cm) long.

A dark-colored animal

The average moose is usually almost black in color. Some are dark brown, while others are rust colored. The color often depends upon the habitat in which the moose lives. Moose that spend most of their time living in the shadows of trees are often very dark in color. If the moose spend much of their time in more open country, they will often be lighter in color. This ability, to adapt its color to its habitat, allows the moose to hide from danger.

Hair around the moose's nostrils, eyes, inner parts of the ears, and its legs is usually light brown or gray. Although albino, or all-white, moose are very rare, a few have been seen in the wild.

The moose's long face ends in a floppy, down-turned nose. Hanging beneath its neck is a long flap of skin and hair called a dewlap. The dewlap is more commonly called a "bell." On bulls, the bell is often a foot (30 cm) long. The bell is quite a bit shorter on cows, but it can still be easily seen. Even the young, called calves, have a small dewlap when they are born.

The hair of the moose is rough and brittle. This is because each hair is filled with tiny air cells. The air cells provide very good insulation during the cold winter months. The moose also has a stiff mane of

14

The hair on a moose is rough and brittle.

hair that runs between its shoulders. The hairs in the mane can be up to ten inches (26 cm) long. This hair stands on end when the moose is alarmed or angry.

Clumsy looking

There is no question that the moose is one of nature's strangest-looking animals. The parts of the animal don't seem to fit together. The front of the moose, including the shoulders and chest, is huge. The back half seems to be made of leftovers. It is much smaller and lower to the ground than the front part of the moose. The moose's legs are long and fragile looking. The belly of the average moose

Moose have long, fragile-looking legs.

stands almost forty inches (103 cm) above the ground. Many fully-grown whitetail deer could stand under a moose with ease!

But all of these parts work together very well. Despite its large size, the moose is very agile and fast. It can turn on a dime! The moose can easily run as fast as thirty-five miles per hour (56 kph). None of the other North American members of the deer family is any faster. The moose can trot for many miles at fifteen miles per hour (24 kph). As many moose hunters know, this huge animal can also vanish without making a sound.

Large feet

The moose has four toes on each hoof, or foot. Each toe is covered with a layer of horny material. The two middle toes on each foot form the main part of each hoof. Each of these toes is about six inches (15 cm) long. Together, the two toes form a heart-shaped track that is about five inches (13 cm) wide.

The other two toes are on the back of the foot. These toes, called dewclaws, are quite a bit smaller than the middle toes. Because they are also higher on the foot than the front toes, they do not make tracks on hard ground. On soft ground, however, the tracks of these back toes can be easily seen.

When the moose is walking through swampy

areas, all of its toes spread apart. This makes it possible for moose to move with ease through the wet areas where it spends most of its time. The track made by a moose is almost twice as big as a track made by either an elk or a caribou.

Huge antlers

As you might expect, the moose has the largest antlers of any living member of the deer family. Only the now extinct Irish elk had larger antlers. The last Irish elk died thousands of years ago. Biologists found the remains of one of these elk in a peat bog in Europe. This elk, which had a body about half the size of today's Alaskan moose, had antlers that were eleven feet (3.4 m) wide. That's an very large "hat!"

Only the bull moose grows antlers. A new set of antlers is grown and shed each year. The bulls grow their first set of antlers during the summer of their second year. The first set of antlers will usually be six-inch "spikes." The next year, the bull will often grow antlers that are forked. The third set of antlers will begin to look like the antlers on a mature bull. These antlers will be slightly flattened, with three or four "points" on each one. As long as the bull stays healthy, the antlers will get larger each year. A mature bull grows "palmated" antlers. These antlers look much like a person's hand. The antlers are much larger, of course. There are many points growing out of a large, flat area.

A bull's antlers are usually biggest when he is twelve to fifteen years old. After that time, the antlers get a bit smaller each year until the moose dies.

The size of a bull's antlers is related to the size of the subspecies. The largest antlers are grown by the largest type of moose. The present world's-record Alaskan moose had antlers that were seventy-seven inches (2 m) wide. The right antler was just under fifty inches (1.3 m) long, and had eighteen points.

A bull's antlers can be huge!

The left antler was the same length and had sixteen points. This pair of antlers weighed just over sixty-three pounds (28.6 kg). The world-record Canada moose's antlers were just over sixty-six inches (1.7 m) wide. The record antlers for the smallest subspecies, the Shiras moose, measured fifty-three inches (1.4 m) across at their widest point.

Even larger antlers have been found. Some Alaskan moose antlers have been found that weighed over eighty-five pounds. One set of Canada moose antlers was seventy-eight inches (2 m) wide. Because world records also take the number of points into account, these antlers didn't qualify as records. They had fewer and smaller points than the world-record antlers.

From velvet to bone

During the time the antlers are growing, they are quite soft. They are made of cartilage during the summer growth period. The growing antlers are covered with "velvet," which is a soft, furry skin. The velvet protects the blood veins that are inside antlers. The antlers can be easily damaged while they are growing. To avoid injury, the bulls stay by them-

Bulls stay to themselves when their antlers are growing and covered with "velvet."

selves and are not very active during this time.

By early fall, the antlers have reached their full size and have stopped growing. The soft cartilage rather quickly turns into very hard bone. At the same time, the velvet loosens up and starts to fall off. The whole process seems to cause the bull's antlers to itch. The bull speeds the shedding of the velvet by rubbing his antlers on tree trunks. This rubbing scrapes a large patch of bark off the trees. The marks left on the trees are called "rubs."

When the bull is finished, his antlers will be shiny and sharp. He will be ready for the coming breeding season. There is only one known reason for the huge antlers. The bulls use their antlers to fight each other for the right to breed the cows.

In early autumn, the "rut" begins! These bulls are fighting for the right to breed cows in the area.

Maturity and life span

Cow moose are mature enough to breed in the fall of their second year, when they are about sixteen months old. However, most cows do not breed for the first time until their third year. Bulls are also able to breed when they are sixteen months old, but the older bulls usually don't let them near the cows. In fact, most bulls don't do any breeding until they are several years old.

Biologists consider moose to be fully mature when they are six years old. But their bodies keep getting larger until they are twelve to fifteen years old. After that time, moose often get a little smaller in size each year until they die.

The average moose lives to be ten to fifteen years old. Many moose are known to have lived for twenty years. Experts think that the maximum possible age is twenty-five years. Other members of the deer family have similiar life spans.

Moose need water

The life of a moose is always tied to water. Without natural areas of water, a moose cannot survive. Moose are animals that browse on brushy twigs and

The favorite food of moose grows in and around water.

leaves. In all areas of their range, their favorite foods are plants and trees that grow in or near water. In most areas of their range, moose escape from summer heat and insects by going into lakes. They also go into rivers and lakes to escape from predators, such as wolves.

Even the Shiras moose, which lives in the mountains, is usually found near water much of the time. This subspecies seeks out mountain lakes and streams.

Moose are very good swimmers. They will often swim across a lake, rather than go around it. Unlike many other animals, they swim high in the water. The air cells in their hair help them float higher in the water. Their head, neck, and back are well out of the water as they swim across a lake or river. Calves are

Calves can swim when they are a few weeks old.

able to swim when they are only a few weeks old. If a calf gets tired while swimming with its mother, it does an interesting thing. The calf puts its head or front feet over its mother's neck. Then the mother tows the calf to shore!

The moose's long legs and large hooves are not an accident. The moose developed these features over thousands of years to help it get around in its watery habitat. The moose can move with amazing speed through bogs and other areas with soft ground.

An expanding range

No one knows for sure how many moose there are in North America today. Many states and provinces are just beginning to count their moose. Counting the moose is not easy, because they live in remote areas where there are no roads.

It is known that Alaska and Ontario each have about eighty thousand moose. Some other provinces might have as many, but no other state does. The best guess of the experts is that there are about half a million moose in North America. This makes the moose about equal in number to the elk.

At the time the first settlers came to North America, most of the moose lived in southern Canada. In the United States, there were good numbers of moose around the Great Lakes and in the New England states. Many moose lived in Pennsylvania and New York. There were a few moose in the northern Rocky Mountain states. There were few, if any, moose in northwestern Canada or Alaska.

Moose have not been able to adapt to man. When many people move into an area where moose live, the moose move away. Because of this habit, most moose disappeared from the settled areas of Canada and the United States. Even in unsettled areas around the Great Lakes, early hunters after meat and hides killed off most of the moose.

An interesting thing began to happen in the late 1800's. Moose expanded their range in the northern Rocky Mountain states of the United States. States such as Idaho, Utah, Montana, and Wyoming have more moose today than ever before.

The moose also expanded their range into northwestern Canada and Alaska in the late 1800's. There are now more moose in this new range than anywhere else in North America.

The experts aren't sure why the moose hadn't moved into these new areas before. Their best guess is that the moose didn't have a reason to move until people started settling near them. Whatever the reason, the new areas were perfect for the moose. The moose thrived like never before.

Recently, states such as Minnesota, Michigan, and Maine have had special programs to build up herds of moose. Each of these states has large areas of wilderness with good moose habitat. The programs have worked very well. The herds have increased to the point where hunting seasons are needed to control the size of the herds.

Without hunting in these states, there would be too many moose on the limited range. Too many moose often leads to the death of a large part of a herd. The deaths are caused by starvation during the winter. Disease also becomes a big problem. Modern game managers use hunting as a tool to prevent this kind of tragedy.

There are probably more moose in North America than there ever have been. Let's now take a closer look at the moose as it goes about its daily business. Hopefully, we'll be able to learn how the moose has done so well.

This small group of moose live on Isle Royal, Michigan.

CHAPTER TWO:

A small home range

The other large members of the deer family in North America, the elk and the caribou, migrate with the seasons from one area to another. The moose does not. In most areas of its range, the moose spends all its time in an area that is about one mile square (2.6 sq. k). In this respect, the moose is like the whitetail deer — the home range of each is about the same. Except during the winter, most moose live by themselves on their home range.

About the only thing that causes a moose to leave its usual home range is a shortage of food. If food is in short supply, a moose will travel until it finds food.

Some bulls of the Alaskan subspecies have a larger home range. On the Kenai Penninsula of Alaska, the bulls leave the low country along the rivers during the summer. They travel several miles to feed on nearby mountains. These bulls also do something else that is different from other moose. While in the mountains they band together, sometimes in rather

When the breeding season starts in the fall, Alaskan moose get together in the low country.

large groups. With the coming of the fall breeding season and cold weather, they rejoin the cows and calves in the low country. Bulls in the Mt. McKinley National Park of Alaska do the same thing. Moose in the Rocky Mountains might move to low country during a bad winter.

The experts are not sure why Alaskan bull moose make this migration. Their best guess is that it has to do with the food supply. They think that there might not be enough food in the low country. The moose have adapted by spreading out during the summer. This would make more food available during the winter, when the moose are all forced into the low country by deep snow.

Food and feeding habits

Moose are animals that browse. They prefer to feed on brushy twigs and leaves. In the wet areas where most moose live, the favorite food seems to be dwarf willow. In forest areas, moose will browse on the tender twigs of birch, aspen, and balsam fir trees. They also like mountain ash, chokecherry, and cottonwood.

This birch tree has been bent over by a moose, so the top branches could be eaten.

Because of its large size, a moose can reach food that is ten feet (3 m) from the ground. If there is shortage of food, a moose will rear up on its back legs and push over a tall bush or small tree. Then the moose can eat the top branches, too!

During the summer, moose feed on water plants most of the time. One of its favorite foods is the leaves of water lilies. A moose will also put its head under the water to reach plants like eelgrass and pondweeds. Moose have even been seen diving completely under the water to reach deep water plants.

The moose's long legs are perfect for wading while feeding on plants in a lake or river. If a moose wants to feed on short grasses on dry ground, it has a problem. Because of its long legs, a moose cannot reach the ground with its mouth while standing up. To get around the problem, the moose will kneel down on its front knees. It will do the same thing to get a drink from a small water hole.

Moose prefer to feed at dawn and again just before sunset. If they are not bothered by people, they might also feed at any hour of the day or night. They spend more time feeding during the winter than at other times of the year. They have to do this to survive in the cold weather.

Like other members of the deer family, moose are "cud chewers." Biologists call these animals ruminants. After eating their fill without chewing, these animals find a safe place to lie down. They then bring the food back up in chunks and chew it. Then the food is reswallowed. This method of eating allows the moose to spend as little time as possible in dangerous, open areas.

Senses and sounds

In order of importance, the moose uses its senses of smell, hearing, and sight to warn of danger. Smell and hearing are, by far, the most important. Both of these senses are highly developed in a moose.

A moose's eyesight is quite poor. In the areas where most moose live, they can't see very far. Moose are usually surrounded by trees and bushes. Experts think that moose never had a need to develop good eyesight. It wouldn't have done them any good if they had.

The moose has one big weakness. Over thousands of years it has learned that danger does not come from across water. Its enemies, mainly wolves, live on the land. So the moose ignores what it sees or hears on the water. The moose does pay attention to what it smells, because the direction of a scent can't be known for sure. This is why I got so close to the moose mentioned in the Introduction.

Moose don't do much "talking." The most common sound is a coughing grunt. Both bulls and cows make this sound to stay in touch with each other. Cows and calves talk to each other with soft bleats. During the mating season, the cows do most of the calling. The cows make a loud, moaning noise. The bulls respond with a short grunt. The sound of a train horn is very close to the moaning made by a cow during the breeding season. Some experts think that this is why bull moose have been known to charge head-on into trains!

Enemies

Wolves and bears are the moose's biggest enemies. These predators kill thousands of moose each year.

The wounds on this calf were caused by a wolf.

Moose often escape from predators by running into the water.

Bears mostly attack moose calves. The most dangerous time for the calves is in the early spring. If there is still deep snow when the bears come out of their dens, many calves might be killed. The huge paws on the bears allow them to move across the top of the snow. The calves often get trapped in the snow as they try to escape. Their legs are too short.

There's no question that wolves kill a lot of moose. But several recent studies have shown that almost all moose killed by wolves are either old, sick, or young calves. Healthy adult moose are usually able to get away from wolves by running into water or deep snow. The moose's long legs allow it to move well in both water and snow. Even if cornered by a large pack of wolves, a healthy moose is usually able to use its hooves to fight off the pack.

The wolf studies also proved another point. By killing the unfit animals, the wolves made it easier for the healthy animals to survive during a food shortage. Healthy animals also make better breeding stock. In the long run, then, wolves are helping the moose survive. It's a good lesson in the balance of nature.

Starvation and diseases

Starvation is the leading cause of natural death among moose. The problem usually occurs in areas where predators have been killed off by people who think they are helping the moose herd. To make matters worse, hunting seasons have often been closed in these same areas.

At first, everything seems fine. With no predators of any kind to control the size of the herd, the numbers of moose increase. However, the herd keeps increasing in size. Before long, the food supply starts to get destroyed. If there is a severe winter ahead, huge numbers of moose will starve. It's a time bomb waiting to go off. This has already happened in Nova Scotia and New Brunswick. In both places, starvation killed most of the moose after hunting seasons were closed.

Parasites of all kinds affect moose. Most parasites do not bother a healthy moose. But many can be fatal if a moose is weakened by a lack of food. The whitetail deer passes on one parasite that is always fatal to a moose — the deer brain worm. The worm is harmless to deer, but the larvae of the worm attack the moose's brain. The larvae get into the moose's habitat through deer droppings.

The rut

The rut, or breeding season, starts in the middle of September. The rut lasts for about six weeks.

During the rest of the year, the bull moose is rather timid. During the rut, the bull's temper is

This bull is in the process of shedding velvet from his antlers just before the start of the rut.

short. The only thing on his mind is finding cows with which to mate. He loses all interest in eating. From his actions, it would appear that he thinks he can handle anything that gets in his way of reaching a mate.

When a bull hears the moaning call of a cow, he moves through his habitat like a tank! He crashes into trees and plows through bushes. Many people have been forced up a tree by an angry bull. During the rut, bulls have attacked cars, bulldozers, and, as already mentioned, trains.

This is what can happen if the antlers of two bulls lock together during a fight.

If two bulls of equal size meet, they lower their heads and charge each other at full speed. The bulls try to push each other to the ground. Sometimes their antlers get locked together. When this happens, both animals will starve to death. The fight usually ends when one bull gives up. Some fights end when one bull gores the other bull to death with his antlers. At no time do smaller bulls take on a larger bull. The smaller bulls leave!

A bull may mate with several cows during the rut, but he stays with only one at a time. Usually the bull and cow are together for about a week. Then the bull goes off to search for another mate.

Calves are born in the spring

The cows carry their calves for about eight months. The calves are born in May or June. Usually one calf will be born to a cow giving birth for the first time. In the following years, the cow will usually have twins. Sometimes triplets are born. The calves usually weigh about thirty pounds (13.6 kg) at birth.

Unlike most other young members of the deer family, the calves do not have spots. They are a solid

A cow watches over her twin calves.

reddish-brown color. Within a few hours, the calf is walking. After a week, it could outrun a person.

The cows are very protective of their calves. They will attack anything that they feel might harm their calves. Cows attack without warning of any kind. Most predators give up as soon as they get slashed with a cow's sharp hooves. Cows have even been known to also attack humans that get near their calves.

Calves stay with their mother through the winter. The cow drives them off when she is ready to give birth again in the early summer. The calves are then on their own. Now they must take care of themselves in their watery habitat. Most of them will do very well. Before long, they will be having calves of their own.

The future can be good

People have always been the moose's worst enemy. In the past, moose were usually forced to leave an area when people moved in. In recent years, people have learned to take care of natural resources, like the moose. If we continue to think wisely, there is no reason why the moose won't continue to do well. The world's largest deer deserves nothing less!

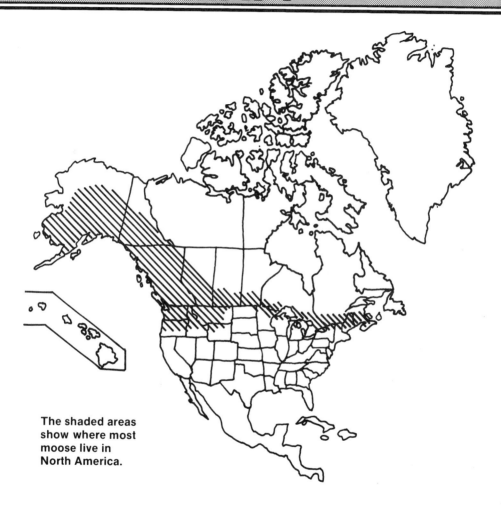

The shaded areas
show where most
moose live in
North America.

INDEX/GLOSSARY:

INDEX/GLOSSARY:

WILDLIFE
HABITS & HABITAT

READ AND ENJOY THE SERIES:

If you would like to know more about all kinds of wildlife, you should take a look at the other books in this series.

You'll find books on bald eagles and other birds. Books on alligators and other reptiles. There are books about deer and other big-game animals. And there are books about sharks and other creatures that live in the ocean.

In all of the books you will learn that life in the wild is not easy. But you will also learn what people can do to help wildlife survive. So read on!